Fidget Spinner

20+ Epic Tricks & Hacks

By JB Books Ltd

The Basic Spinning

The Basic Spinning trick is the simplest trick, where you only spin the fidget spinner between your fingers (first and second finger).

Step by step:

- Put the fidget spinner between your first and second finger
- Spin the fidget spinner

BASIC SPINNING

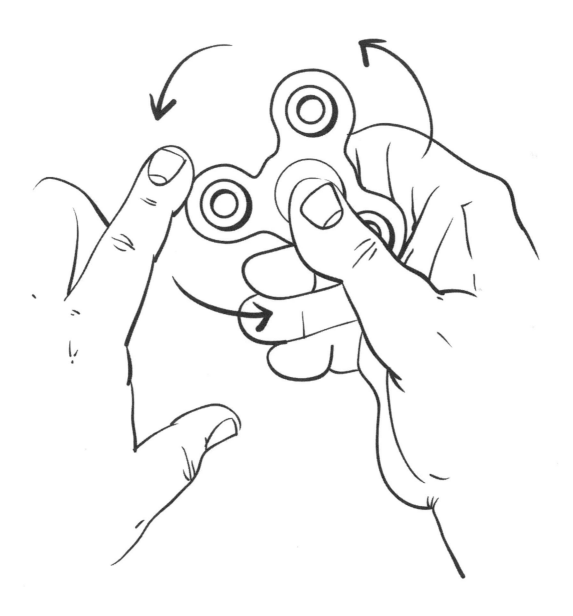

The Pencil Trick

The Pencil trick is an easy trick to do. You have to put a pencil through the middle hole of your fidget spinner, spin it and watch it twirl.

Step by step:

- Put a pencil through the middle hole in your fidget spinner
- Spin the fidget spinner

PENCIL TRICK

1.)

2.)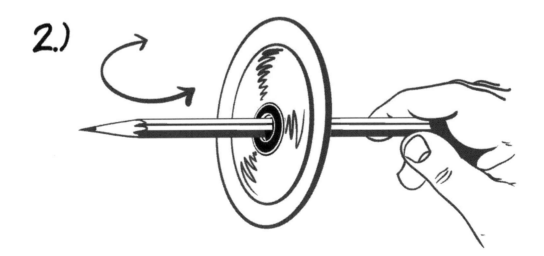

The Table Spin

The Table Spin is one of the easiest tricks. You have to place the fidget spinner simply on the table and spin it as fast as you can.

Step by step:

- Put the fidget spinner on the table
- Spin the fidget spinner

TABLE SPIN

1.)

2.)

3.)

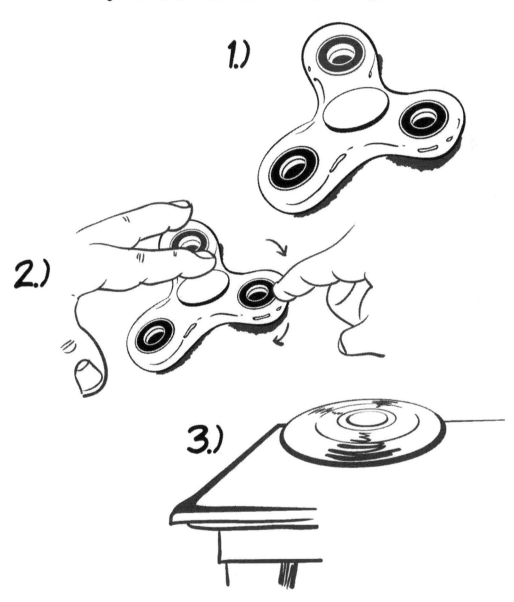

The Hat Trick

The Hat Trick is one of the hardest tricks with the fidget spinners. Spin the spinner between your fingers and throw it through the air onto your baseball hat so it keeps spinning onto it.

Step by step:

- Put the fidget spinner between your first and second finger
- Spin the fidget spinner
- Throw the fidget spinner in the air onto your baseball hat
- Keep the fidget spinner spinning

HAT TRICK

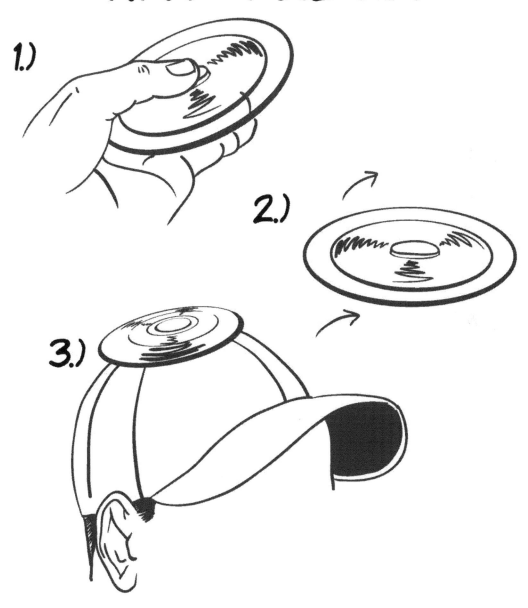

1.)

2.)

3.)

The Nose Spinner

The Nose Spinner trick is again a little harder to do. Like the name says, you have to place the fidget spinner on the top of your nose and spin it.

Step by step:

- Put the fidget spinner on the tip of your nose
- Spin the fidget spinner

NOSE SPINNER

1.)

2.)

3.)

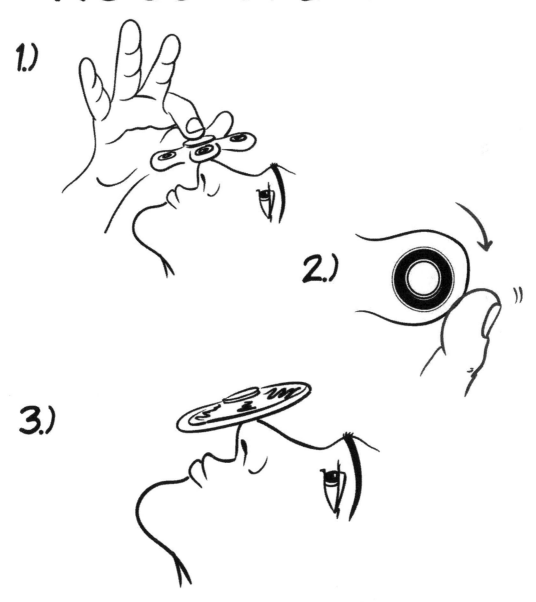

The Double Spinner

The Double spinner trick is the same like the Basic spinning trick, expect you are performing it with two fidget spinners. Take a fidget spinner in each hand and spin them at the same time.

Step by step:

- Put two fidget spinners between your first and second finger in each hand
- Spin the fidget spinners

DOUBLE SPINNER

1.)

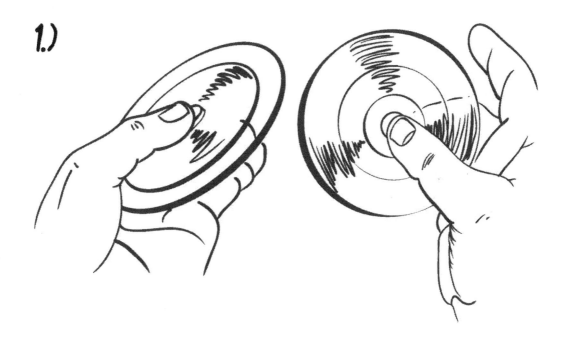

The UFO Trick

The UFO trick requires some preparations of you. First you have to attach a short string on your fidget spinner. The you hold the string so the fidget spinner is hanging and you spin it, so it looks like you are holding an UFO.

Step by step:

- Attach short string on the fidget spinner
- Hold the string so the fidget spinner is hanging
- Spin the fidget spinner

UFO TRICK

1.)

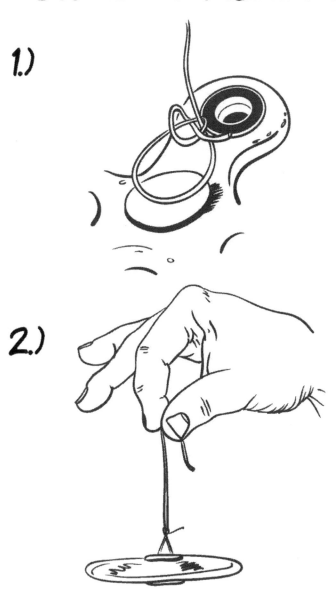

2.)

The Edge Trick

To perform the Edge trick you need a fidget spinner and an object with sharp edges. First you normally spin the fidget spinner and then you put it on the corner of an object. Try to keep the balance of the fidget spinner while it's spinning.

Step by step:

- Put the fidget spinner between your first and second finger
- Spin the fidget spinner
- Place the fidget spinner on the corner of an object
- Keep the balance of the fidget spinner

EDGE TRICK

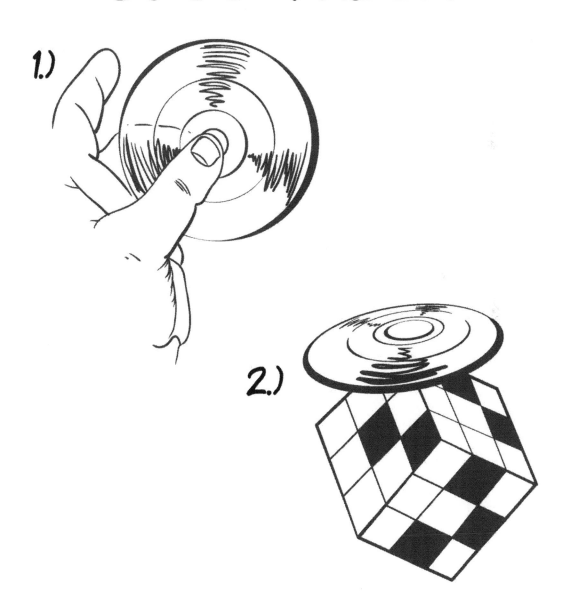

1.)

2.)

The Spinner Stack Trick

To perform the Spinner stack trick you need three fidget spinners and two round objects, like oranges. First you have to place one fidget spinner on the table, then put an orange on top of it, again one fidget spinner on the top of the orange and so on, so you get a stack of fidget spinners and oranges.

Step by step:

- Place the fidget spinner on the floor/table
- Put the orange on the top of the first fidget spinner
- Place second fidget spinner on the top of the orange
- Put second orange on the top of the second fidget spinner
- Place third fidget spinner on the top of the second orange
- Spin all the fidget spinner

SPINNER STACK TRICK

1.)

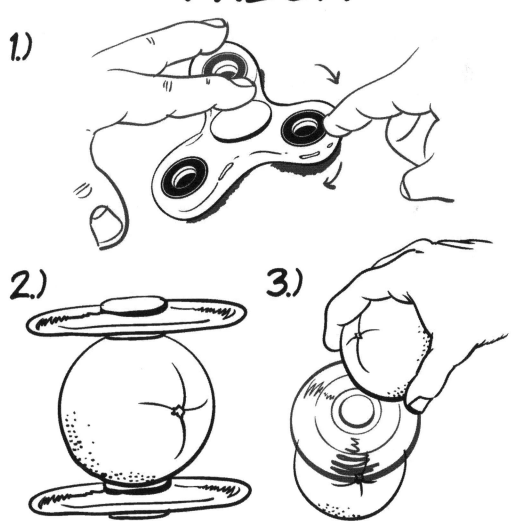

2.)

3.)

The Backhand Flip

The Backhand flip trick is little bit harder trick to do. First you normally spin the fidget spinner between your fingers, the you toss it to the back of your hand and then back to your fingers, everything while the fidget spinner is spinning.

Step by step:

- Put the fidget spinner between your first and second finger
- Spin the fidget spinner
- Toss the fidget spinner on the back of your hand
- Toss the fidget spinner back to your fingers

BACKHAND FLIP

1.)

2.)

3.)

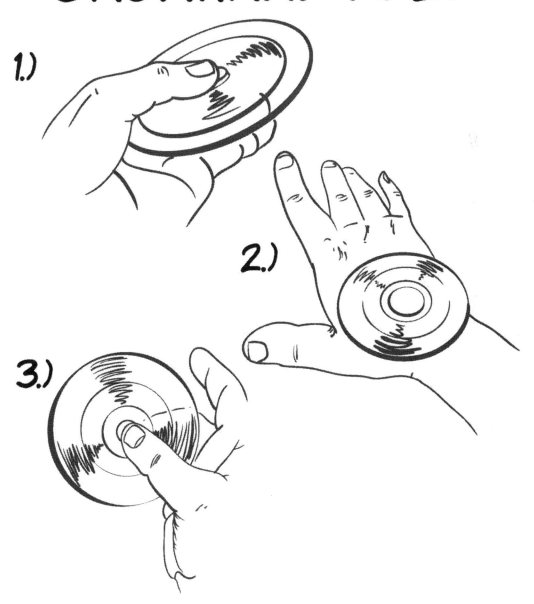

The Hot Potato

The Hot Potato trick is a little harder to do. You have to spin the fidget spinner in one hand and toss it through the air in the other hand, so it looks like you are handling a hot potato.

Step by step:

- Put the fidget spinner between your first and second finger
- Spin the fidget spinner
- Throw the fidget spinner through the air in the other hand
- Throw the fidget spinner through the air back in the first hand

HOT POTATO

1.)

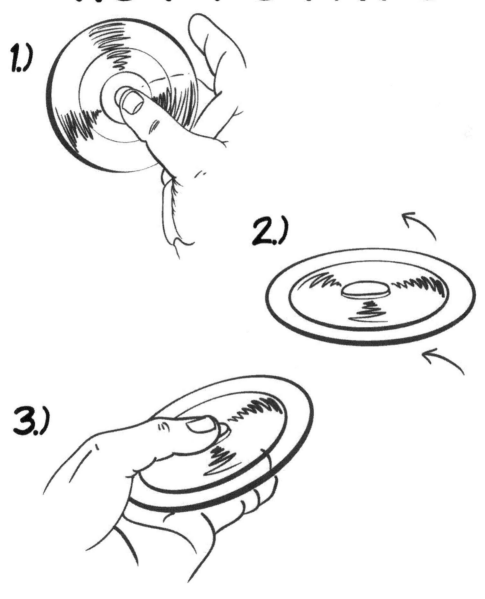

2.)

3.)

The Sky Toss

The sky toss trick is a little harder to do. After you normally spin the fidget spinner between your hands, you have to throw the fidget spinner up in the air and catch it while it is still spinning.

Step by step:

- Put the fidget spinner between your first and second finger
- Spin the fidget spinner
- Throw the fidget spinner up in the air
- Catch the fidget spinner back with your fingers while it's spinning

SKY TOSS

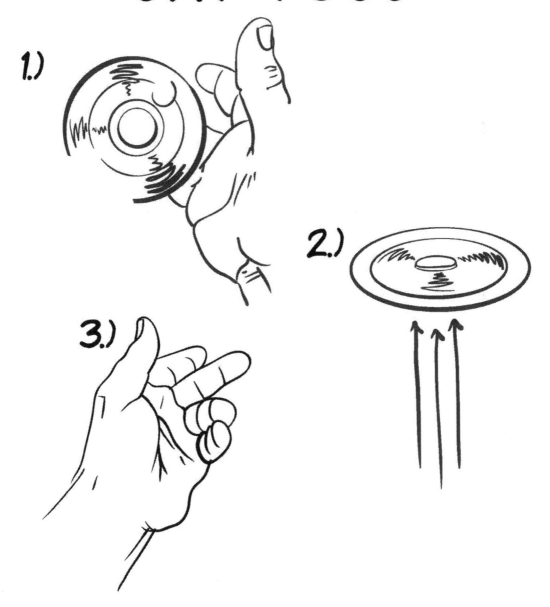

The Football Trick

The Football trick is semi-hard trick to do. The goal of the trick is that you can manage keep the fidget spinner spinning while you are handling it from you hand to your knee and back in you hand.

Step by step:

- Put the fidget spinner between your first and second finger
- Spin the fidget spinner
- Place the fidget spinner on your knee while it's spinning
- Take the fidget spinner back in your hand while it's spinning

FOOTBALL TRICK

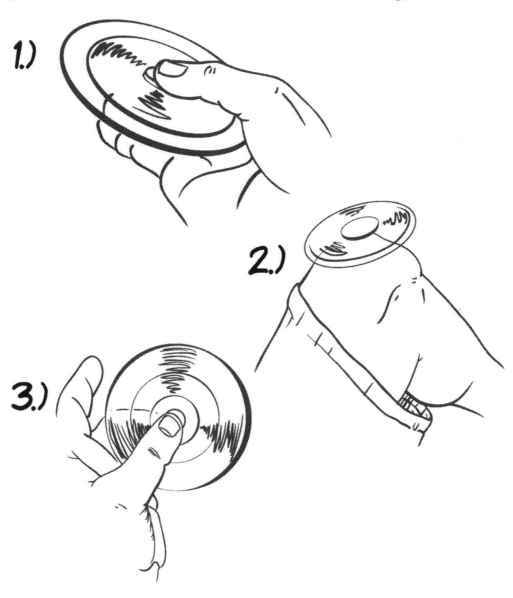

1.)

2.)

3.)

The Under the Leg Trick

In the Under the leg trick you have to spin the fidget spinner in one hand and pass it under your leg in the other hand, while the fidget spinner is spinning this whole time.

Step by step:

- Put the fidget spinner between your first and second finger
- Spin the fidget spinner
- Lift up your leg
- Pass the fidget spinner in your other hand while it's spinning

UNDER THE LEG TRICK

1.)

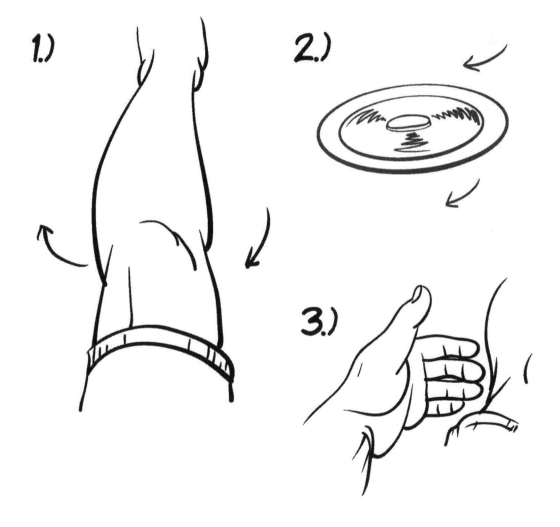

2.)

3.)

The Over the Back Trick

The over the back trick is again pretty hard to do. You have to spin the fidget spinner with one hand, throw it over your back and catch it with the other hand.

Step by step:

- Put the fidget spinner between your first and second finger
- Spin the fidget spinner
- Throw the fidget spinner over your back
- Catch the fidget spinner with the other hand

OVER THE BACK TRICK

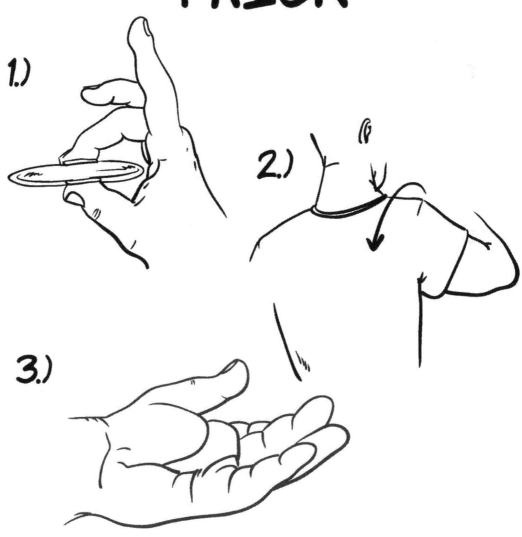

1.)

2.)

3.)

The Twirling Trick

The Twirling trick is again a little harder to perform. After you normally spin the fidget spinner you throw it in the air and catch it only with one finger.

Step by step:

- Put the fidget spinner between your first and second finger
- Spin the fidget spinner
- Throw the fidget spinner in the air
- Catch the fidget spinner only with one finger

TWIRLING TRICK

1.)

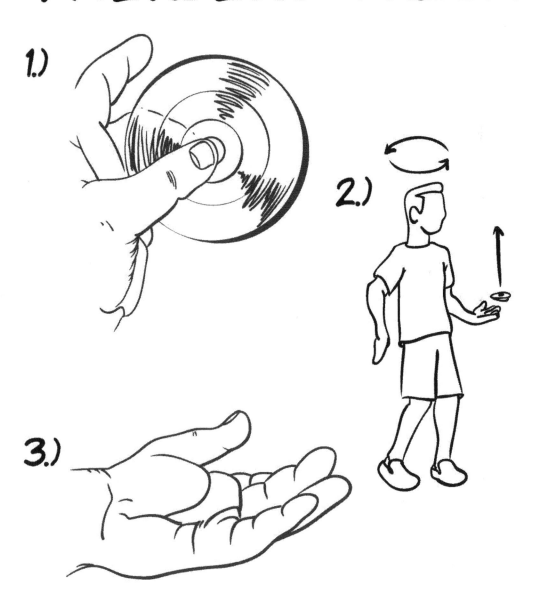

2.)

3.)

The Phasing Fidget

The Phasing fidget is one of the hardest tricks to do. You have to simultaneously spin two fidget spinners, one in each hand, and pass them across each other while both fidget spinners are spinning.

Step by step:

- Put the first fidget spinner between your first and second finger in one hand
- Put the second fidget spinner between first and second finger in other hand
- Spin both fidget spinners
- Pass fidget spinners across each other while they are spinning

PHASING FIDGET

1.)

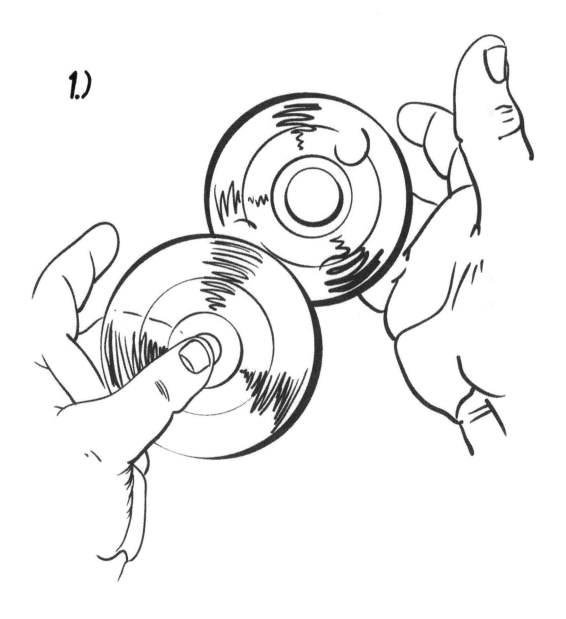

Dancing Spinners

For perform the Dancing spinners trick you need two fidget spinners and two small magnets. You have to put those two magnets on your fidget spinners, one magnet on each spinner. Because of the magnets the fidget spinners will rotate together and it will look like they are dancing.

Step by step:

- Place two fidget spinners on the floor/table
- Put one magnet on each fidget spinner

DANCING SPINNERS

1.)

2.)

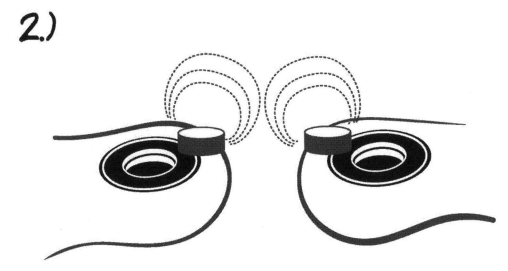

The Parallel Trick

To perform the Parallel trick you need two fidget spinners and one magnet. With the help of the magnet you put two fidget spinners together and rotate them simultaneously.

Step by step:

- Put the magnet on the back of the first fidget spinner
- Put the second fidget spinner on the other side of the magnet, so you have a magnet between two fidget spinner
- Spin both fidget spinners simultaneously

PARALLEL TRICK

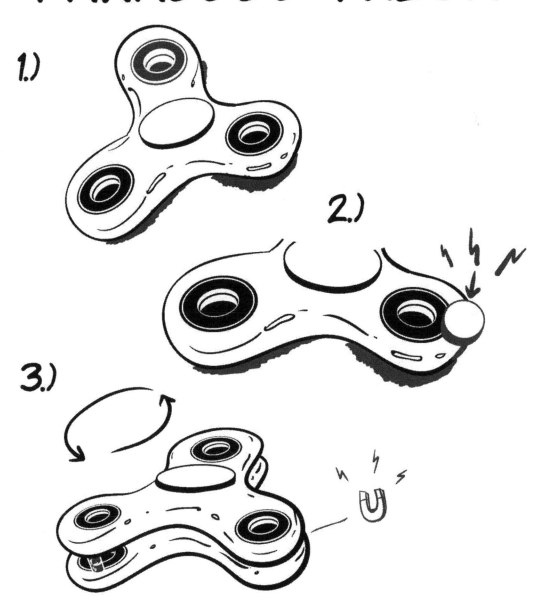

1.)

2.)

3.)

The Ten Fingers Spin

In the Ten fingers spin trick you have to use all of your fingers in both hands. The goal of the trick is that you spin the fidget spinner from first finger of one hand to the last finger of the other hand, so you have to put through all ten fingers.

Step by step:

- Put the fidget spinner between your first and second finger
- Spin the fidget spinner
- While it's spinning move the fidget spinner from finger to finger

TEN FINGER SPIN

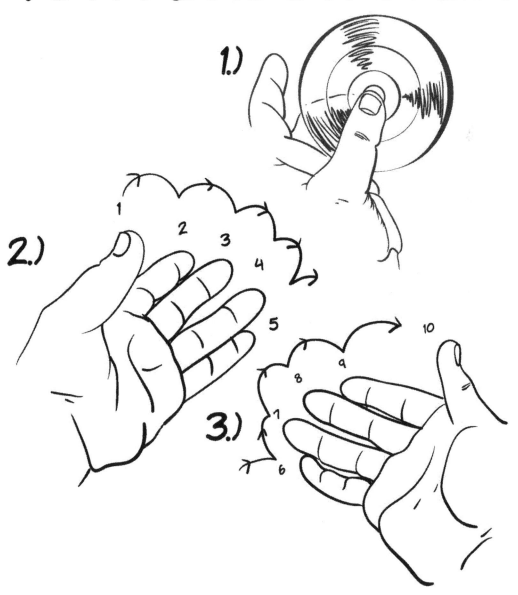

Fun Fidget Spinning Facts

1. A fidget spinner is basically a stress relief toy. It's made up of a ball bearing surrounded by a circular pad with "blades" which spin around the bearing.
2. Catherine Hettinger, the inventor who first patented the toy in 1997, could not afford to renew the patent in 2005. The fee was $400, at that time, so Catherine considered this to be too much of a luxury for a "useless" toy.
3. The fidget spinner was initially developed in the 90's to help people who have trouble focusing, and those with ADHD, autism, or anxiety.
4. Publications and online stores marketed the toy as a calming tool to stay focused, or something to help relieve stress, but this is not clinically proven.
5. As the fidget spinner spun its way all over the world, more companies have started shipping or even producing these little toys. If you go on amazon.com the price may start at $2 and end at almost $700 per single spinner.
6. The fidget spinner can also explode. In the U.S. a Bluetooth-enabled spinner caught on fire while charging.
7. The record for the longest spin was set by Jeffrey Fred. He managed to spin the toy for 6 minutes 52 seconds. The record hasn't been broken yet.
8. Average spin of a fidget spinner is 104 seconds.
9. Nobody knows why the fidget spinners are now all of the sudden so popular, as they have been around for 20 years.
10.   It's so popular, it's banned in some schools.

Made in the USA
Lexington, KY
12 September 2017